CATCH
Attracting and Connecting Visitors

More CATCH Resources:

Catch Workbook (9780687656646)
Catch a New Life (9780687656745)
Catch DVD (9780687656844)
Catch Planning Kit (9780687656943)

CATCH
Attracting and Connecting Visitors

DEBI WILLIAMS NIXON with ADAM HAMILTON

Abingdon Press
Nashville

CATCH:
Attracting and Connecting Visitors

This book is printed on acid-free, recycled paper.

09 10 11 12 13 14 15 16 17 18 – 10 9 8 7 6 5 4 3 2 1

MANUFACTURED IN THE UNITED STATES OF AMERICA

Contents

Go Fish! Series

As Jesus was walking beside the Sea of Galilee, he saw two brothers, Simon called Peter, and his brother Andrew. They were casting a net into the lake—for they were fishermen. "Come, follow me," Jesus said, "and I will send you out to fish for people." At once they left their nets and followed him. —*Matthew 4:18-20 (TNIV)*

Go Fish! is a card game designed for children four years and over. The game consists of 40 playing cards with different types of brightly colored fish (pink, red, orange, purple, brown, green, blue, yellow, white, or gray) on each individual card. The goal is to get a set of four cards of the same color of fish and lay them down in front of you. The person who gets the most sets of same-colored fish is the winner of the game.

A player will ask other players if they have a certain color fish card in their hand and if they do, they have to surrender it to the person requesting it. If they don't have it they will say Go Fish! and the player requesting the card will have to draw a card from the central stack.

Many young children love to play this game, and I have played it for hours with my young grandchildren. The principle of the game is simple. If you cannot get the card you need from another player you have to Go Fish! which means you have to reach out and hope to draw the card you need.

The Go Fish! Series is about encouraging followers of Jesus to Go Fish!, which means to reach out to the people in their communities in compassionate, loving ways so that people without any current interest in following Jesus might want to come and become a part of particular faith community.

Jesus practiced the same principle when he called the brothers Peter and Andrew to become his first followers. Peter and Andrew were fishermen on the Sea of Galilee. They would get in their boat each day, go out to the deep part of the lake, throw out their nets, and hopefully pull in a catch of fish.

Peter and Andrew did not sit in their boat near the shore and wait for the fish to come and jump into their boat. They knew that they had to go out to the deep water in order to catch the fish and bring them into their boat. They had to reach out to catch the fish; the fish wouldn't automatically come to them. They had to Go Fish!

In a similar way, congregations need to go out into their neighborhoods and communities in loving and serving ways if they want to invite more persons to become followers of Jesus who make a positive difference in the world. Congregational leaders need to learn how to Go Fish! in their communities.

Just as we do not expect fish to come and simply jump into a boat because it is there, we cannot expect that somehow people will simply come and jump into our congregations because we are there.

Our goal is not just to enable congregations to grow in participation and membership. Our goal is that congregations will become vital centers of loving service for the spiritual and personal needs of the people of their communities so that the world will be transformed into a compassionate, just, inclusive, and Christ-like community.

The ultimate goal of the Go Fish! Series is to be used by God for the transformation of the people in our communities from fear to faith, from complacency to compassion, and from greed to generosity. Our hope is that more and more people will become followers of Jesus, who is still at work in transforming and redeeming our world.

Kent Millard, Senior Pastor, St. Luke's United Methodist Church

Acknowledgments

Sharing the story of the way God is at work in the life of a congregation is an incredible privilege. I feel such privilege to share ideas and stories of The United Methodist Church of the Resurrection—a church started in 1990, with a dream of reaching non and nominally religious people in the south Johnson County, Kansas area. The church started with only four people and is now a growing congregation of over 15,000 members on the journey to become deeply committed Christians who know, love, and serve God.

In this book I have reflected on our experiences in implementing the evangelism practices of Church of the Resurrection and drawn upon the ideas of my Senior Pastor, Adam Hamilton through his leadership and from his book Leading Beyond the Walls. It is a privilege to serve with him. I am thankful for the many ways he has invested in the development of his team and in me.

I want to thank the staff and lay leaders at the Church of the Resurrection who demonstrate and live the principles outlined in this book. Because of their efforts, sacrifices, and hospitality, thousands of people have become followers of Jesus Christ. For the last nineteen years they've "fished for people."

I am grateful for my husband, my two children, family, and friends for their role both in the ministries at the church, and in the work of writing this book.

Finally, I thank God for the privilege of seeking to "catch" persons as fishers of people and for the opportunity to share the story of how this is lived out at Church of the Resurrection.

Introduction
Relentlessly Outward Focused

For the Son of Man came to seek and to save what was lost. —Luke 19:10

The very first week at Church of the Resurrection, our senior pastor Adam Hamilton, preached these words, "We're going to be focused on people outside of our doors. We're going to be concerned about the non and nominally religious more than ourselves." We had fervor around this principle and each charter member was focused on our mission. And then it happened. Four weeks later, during a meeting of the leadership team, one of our members said, "Pastor Adam, I love our church the size we are now. I love how close we are. I hope we never get any bigger than this." As Adam looked around the room, he noticed that everyone was nodding their head in agreement. All of the leaders—the leaders!—were saying, "Yes, yes, I hope we never get any bigger than this. It's wonderful how small and close we are." Adam thought, "How did this happen?" Just four weeks before he had preached about our mission—we were going to exist for all of the people out in the world who didn't know Christ—and in just those four weeks, our church had turned inward.

Does this happen in your church as well? Have you discovered how easy it is to become so close with those inside the walls that you lose concern for those outside the walls of the church? We can easily become comfortable, like a close-knit family. But the relationships can actually serve as a barrier that keeps people out. If a visitor shows up, everyone "in the family" is so close to one another, talking and sharing inside stories, that the visitor feels like an outsider from the minute he or she walks in. Or, the worship service itself may communicate that it's only for people who already know what to do—not for those who may be attending church for the first time ever.

The truth is that very few of us would admit that we are this church. We think we are friendly enough. We'll often defend our friendliness and ignore the fact that visitors cannot find a place in our communities. In reality, everything the church does is really designed for the benefit of the inside group.

Looking Out

When we decide that evangelism is essential, we become churches that are relentlessly outward focused. The outward-focused church looks at everything it does and asks, "How can this help us reach non and nominally religious people?" and "Would a first-time visitor have a sense of what is important here?"

Unfortunately, it is easy for churches to become inward focused and more interested on the people inside the walls of the church, neglecting those outside the walls of the church. Every church will naturally tend to focus on those inside the community, so the leader must constantly remind the church why they exist—for those who do not yet know the love of God.

Jesus knew his purpose. Luke 19:10 tells us that *"the Son of Man came to seek and to save what was lost."* He did not focus only on those who had already decided to follow him, but instead demonstrated an outward approach. *"Jesus went through all the towns and villages, teaching in their synagogues, proclaiming the good news of the kingdom, and healing every disease and sickness. When he saw the crowds, he had compassion on them, because they were harassed and helpless, like sheep without a shepherd"* (Matthew 9:35-36). If the church is the body of Christ, we must have the same heart as Christ. The heart of Christ was compassion for lost people. Our churches exist to proclaim the good news to lost people. If we take Jesus' teachings seriously, then as a church we have to consider whether we are focused inward on the "found" or are we out there fishing for people?

Fishing for People

Pastor Kent Millard talks about evangelism in terms of fishing. He says that in order to catch fish you have to go to where they are. If Christians are to be fishers of people, then they have to learn how to fish. They have to learn the fishing conditions in their areas. They have to check the weather. They have to own the right equipment and learn the proper techniques. Sometimes churches forget this and just hang out their "OPEN" sign and hope that people will pour in.

The fact that you're reading this right now probably means that you're working on becoming an outward-focused congregation. You want non and nominally religious people to find a home in your church. You want to have a church full of members who are more focused on bringing people in than on getting their favorite pew and parking spot each week.

The Catch approach to evangelism is a tool to help you cast a wide net in your community, to look outward and find out how you might connect to those who are not already inside your walls. In this book, we'll talk about clarifying your mission, marketing your church, creating worship that non-religious people find a place in, becoming a welcoming community, and creating a clear path from first-time visitor to thriving member.

An aimless expedition without the proper gear will lead to frustration, burn out, and probably bear no fruit from the effort—but what would you expect? On the other hand, an intentional effort to chart a course, research your surroundings and conditions, choose the right "bait," and learn what to do when you actually hook something leads to a successful outing and presumably a great catch!

Our prayer for you as you read this book is that you will take on the challenge of turning your congregation outward and taking seriously Jesus' command to go and fish for people—and that your "Catch" is so great you'll need a bigger net!

Chapter One
Three Important Questions

I must preach the good news of the kingdom of God to the other towns also, because that is why I was sent. —Luke 4:43

One summer I watched my teenage daughter and a few of her friends set out to catch fish from the dock of our lake house. They gathered a few fishing poles, loaded into the paddleboat, and headed out about thirty-five feet from the dock. After about an hour of casting and reeling in nothing, they returned frustrated, discouraged, and declared that fishing was "a waste of time and boring." When I asked what kind of bait they were using, they responded that they didn't have any bait. They thought the fish would just bite on the hook. I probed further and asked what kind of fish they had hoped to catch. The response was one of puzzlement. What do you mean "What kind of fish? Fish, of course." They had simply set out to catch "fish" without clarity of purpose, knowledge of the environment, or understanding of what might be needed to actually catch fish.

Sometimes the church's biggest hindrance to evangelism is a lack of clarity of purpose, knowledge of the community and needs of the people, and an understanding of what might be needed to reach them. As the leader, you must cast a clear vision for the calling and purpose for which God has called your church. Jesus was clear about his purpose. He was resolute on doing what his Father had called him to do. Even at the young age of twelve, he was clear that he was to be about his Father's business. He said to them, *"Why were you searching for me? Did you not know that I must be in my Father's house?"* (Luke 2:49). Jesus stayed focused on his purpose throughout his ministry as seen in Luke 4:42-43. At the beginning of his ministry, we read in Scripture of crowds approaching him while in Galilee asking him to stay. But to them he stated clearly his purpose, *"I must proclaim the good news of the kingdom of God to the other cities also; for I was sent for this purpose"* (Luke 4:43). Even as he was on his way to Jerusalem approaching the cross, Scripture tells us he knew exactly what he had to do. *"As the time approached for him to be taken up to heaven, Jesus resolutely set out for Jerusalem"* (Luke 9:51, TNIV). Growing churches are clear on their purpose and resolutely set out to work with God to accomplish that purpose.

To have a clear purpose as a church means you know why you exist. The purpose at our church is clearly understood by everyone in our congregation and we all agree upon it. Our purpose statement defines everything we do: *To build a Christian community where non-religious and nominally-religious people are becoming deeply committed Christians.* Every person in leadership, and we hope, most of our members, can recite this purpose statement from memory. Our purpose statement is written in twelve-inch letters in our narthex so that all who enter or leave our building are reminded of why we exist. Visually, we have four tapestries that hang behind the chancel in our sanctuary. Each tapestry illustrates a scene from Jesus' life and ministry: his birth (Luke 2:1-20), his forgiveness of a sinful woman (Luke 7:36-50), his ministry to a tax collector (Luke 19:1-10), and his resurrection (Luke 24:1-9). The scenes show how Jesus reached out in love, offering forgiveness and salvation to the people society had abandoned, ostracized, or ignored—the least, the last, and the lost. The tapestries serve as a visual reminder of our purpose, to reach out to the non and nominally religious in our community.

After we had established a clear purpose, we had some more work to do. Before we made the phone calls inviting people to our first worship service, we needed to answer some key questions, the answers to which would drive everything else we did and help us live out our purpose statement. Our pastor knew it was his responsibility to cast a clear, compelling vision, and that without a deep conviction about the responses to these questions the church would flounder. He wrestled with these three questions in order to help us catch his vision for our church:

• Why do people need Jesus Christ?

16

• Why do people need the church?
• Why do people need your particular church?

Why Do People Need Jesus Christ?

Here we don't mean to ask why Jesus Christ would be a nice thing for people to have in their lives. Rather, we ask, why do people need him? You are making disciples of Jesus Christ and inviting people to follow him. You are inviting them to change their lives and commit or surrender to Jesus Christ. So why do people need Jesus Christ?

We need Jesus Christ because he alone satisfies the deepest longings of the human heart. Persons will not find their deepest needs met when they go to the shopping mall or in another person. The need for unconditional grace and mercy, the need to believe that there's hope for the future, and the need to know that in the darkest moments of our lives the darkness will not prevail, are met only in Jesus Christ.

Jesus said, *"I am the resurrection and the life. Anyone who believes in me will live, even though they die"* (John 11:25, TNIV). He gives us hope when we have been diagnosed with a terminal illness. When we are struggling with relationships and marriage, we can find no other hope than in the one who changes hearts. The great problems in our world—racism, poverty, and war— at their core are all spiritual problems. These problems have to do with the human condition that is broken in us, which can only be addressed by Jesus Christ. You must be absolutely convinced of this if you are going to reach people for Jesus Christ.

In *Leading Beyond the Walls (Abingdon Press, 2002),* Adam Hamilton shares,

Jesus Christ is the solution to the deepest longings of the human heart. He is the answer to the most serious problems that plague our society. When Jesus is Lord and the Holy Spirit enters the heart of the believer, we find the empty places filled, and the dark sides of our soul transformed. We are in the process of becoming 'new creatures in Christ.' Why do people need Christ? Because without him we will always be lost and our lives will never realize their God-given potential.

He opens the door to a whole new world for us. He enriches every life he touches. He changes the world one person at a time, as his kingdom expands the globe (pages 22-23).

We must be able to communicate the answer to this question to people who are unconvinced of their need for Jesus Christ. We must be able to communicate in a way that is compelling to them, not just compelling to us. But first, we must believe it. It must be something we so believe in that when we are sharing it with people, they can see it in our eyes and hear it in our tone of voice. We must fundamentally believe that Jesus Christ is essential for being fully human. He is the answer to the deepest longings of our soul.

Why Do People Need the Church?

This question is important because you are not only inviting people to follow Jesus but to become a part of a church. There are those who believe in Jesus Christ but do not believe they need a church. Some are distrustful of organized religion. Some believe the church is narrow-minded and comprised of hypocrites, that all we want is their money. Others feel like the church is irrelevant, out of touch, and boring. So, if these people are not convinced they need organized religion, how do you persuade them that they need the church? The New Testament shows us that church is not our idea. The church was Jesus' idea. He organized his followers and said, *"On this rock I will build my church, and the gates of Hades will not prevail against it"* (Matthew 16:18). Church leaders must have a fundamental conviction about the absolute necessity of the church if they are going to lead the church.

In fact, some research studies in the United States look at the effects that being a part of a church community has on physical health. These studies demonstrate that people live longer and that they're healthier in old age when they have a family, a church family, than those who don't have a church family.

Adam Hamilton shares this story about why we need the church:

When I was a child, a family in my neighborhood was among the first to purchase a Japanese car. It was a Honda. It was a little, tiny car. There were four of us kids in the neighborhood who decided to play a trick on the people who owned the car. So we went out in the middle of the night and we each took one end of the car and we picked it up and turned the car completely sideways in front of their house. There was virtually no way to move it the next day. They couldn't drive it because we moved it sideways. There was no way to get it out. I'm not suggesting you should do this. But this demonstrated to me the power of four people all working together with the same goal. And it paints a picture for me to show what can happen when Christians get together to work toward Christ's goals. And that is part of the power of the church—Christians working together to do what no one of us can do by ourselves.

We are convinced that we can never be the kind of Christians God wants us to be without other Christians. We need each other. God gave each of us different spiritual gifts. I need your spiritual gifts and you need my spiritual gifts. I need you to hold me accountable and you need me to hold you accountable for growing in Christ. I need to pray for you and I need you to pray for me. When I am sick and in the hospital, I need you to come visit me and when you are sick and in the hospital you need me to come visit you. As a church body, we are able to support one another even in our darkest times.

Through community, we have the opportunity to serve others. As a church, we pray for and care for one another. Right after our family had joined the church, my husband was still trying to be a weekend flag football warrior and suffered a full Achilles tendon tear while playing an out-of-state tournament. We arrived back in Kansas City, and he was sent to the hospital for immediate surgery. When we arrived at the hospital, there was a small group of people from the church, whom we had only barely met, waiting to pray for us before Reed went into surgery. They sat with me then and continued to visit during his hospital stay. They brought meals for the next month and were such a blessing to me as I cared for our two toddlers and for Reed. To this day I have never forgotten the blessing of a church community.

As a church body, we are able to support one another even in our darkest times. When one of our members lost his job, his small group was there to support and encourage him. When the wife of one of our members was killed in a tragic accident, her ministry team surrounded her family with love and care. When a woman confessed that she was addicted to sleeping pills, it was her pastor who got her the help she needed, while the support groups at church helped her stay accountable and drug free. One of our pastors received a call to go to the ICU where a man had been told his wife would not survive. When the pastor arrived, the man's small group was already in the room surrounding him with love and support. As his fellow believers, they were there carrying him through the darkest time in his life. This is what it means to be the church.

We also need the church because we were made to worship God together. In the midst of worship and singing with other Christians, I experience the presence of the Holy Spirit. Something happens to me when I hear the word of God preached; God speaks to me through the proclamation of the Word. Jesus said that where a few people are gathered, he is there (Matthew 18:20). I experience Christ just by being surrounded by his church gathered in worship. Together we are part of something so much bigger than any one of us. Together we can accomplish more for God than any of us can do by ourselves.

Why Do People Need Your Particular Church?
Assuming that you have the answer to why people need Jesus Christ and why they need the church, the third question to ask yourself is why people need your particular church? This was a very important question for us. When our church was starting there were dozens of other churches starting at about the same time. So why start another church? What is it that we offer that might reach someone that the other churches might not reach? We needed to be clear about what was special about our particular congregation. Not better than others, but what is unique about us? What are we going to be known for?

We determined that our church would be about reaching "thinking people" in our community by preaching sermons that spoke both to the heart and to the mind. We would offer great programs for children and youth, and we would equip our people to be salt and light in our community through service and outreach. We were also committed to excellence, and employed a "whatever it takes" approach to ministry.

During the first years of our church, a family moved to our community with a severely handicapped son. After their first visit, our pastor went to "mug" them as part of our follow-up strategy for first-time visitors (more on that in Chapter Four). During the visit, they told him that although they had enjoyed the service, we could not be their church home. When the pastor probed further, they said we were just too small and would not be able to minister to them as a family because of the special needs of their son. They talked more about what might be needed, and the pastor came back to the church the following Sunday and cast a vision asking if we were willing to do "whatever it takes" to be their church family. We mobilized our small church at that time to develop a ministry that would allow the family to worship weekly and attend Sunday school, while their son received personalized one-on-one care. Now, "Matthew's Ministry" is a thriving ministry and many of the children have now grown into adults who are ministering back to the congregation through a new bakery they call "Sonshine Bakery." They prepare pastries to sell in our café and other local coffee shops. From that "whatever it takes to be your church family" attitude, we now have a weekly ministry that serves over one hundred families in our community. We knew that there was a need for this kind of church and if we could become it, we would reach people in our community that no one else was reaching.

Armed with the answers to these questions, convicted and persuaded that people needed Jesus Christ, they need the church, and they need your particular church, you are ready to put the Catch principles to work and go fish for people.

To read more about Adam Hamilton's responses to the "three questions," look in chapter one of his book Leading Beyond the Walls.

Chapter Two
Attracting People in Your Community

As Jesus walked beside the Sea of Galilee, he saw Simon and his brother Andrew casting a net into the sea—for they were fishermen. "Come, follow me," Jesus said, "and I will send you out to fish for people."
—Mark 1:16-17 (TNIV)

My father-in-law is an avid fisherman. He has learned that certain bait attracts a certain type of fish, but not another. He loves to fish in the local lakes in our area which are teeming with catfish, perch, crappie, and bass. Stinkbait, breadballs, and even a simple worm are tasty treats for catfish or a perch. But if you want to reel in a bass, he'll tell you that none of these options is effective. To catch the attention of a bass requires a live minnow or a shiny spinner lure. Crappie also like minnows, but not in the same way as the bass. In order to catch a bass, the minnow or lure is cast toward the shore in the shallow water where the bass feed. To catch crappie, you cast the minnow deep in the water and keep it still until the crappie takes notice.

Fishermen know that one single style of bait is not effective at attracting the variety of fish in a particular lake or body of water. You need a tackle box filled with a variety of baits, lures, and weights. As churches, one of the keys to becoming more effective at reaching people in our communities is to increase the tools in our evangelism tackle box. Too often, a church uses one style of reaching people, maybe a weekly ad in the newspaper, maybe a yellow page ad, or maybe the sign in front of your church. All are good methods, but alone they are not enough to attract the various unchurched people in your community.

Mark 1:16-17 (TNIV) says, *"As Jesus walked beside the Sea of Galilee, he saw Simon and his brother Andrew casting a net into the sea—for they were fishermen. 'Come, follow me,' Jesus said, 'and I will send you out to fish for people.'* Note that the fishermen Jesus called were not fishermen for hobby or sport, they fished to survive. It was their livelihood. Too often, churches view evangelism as important, but not necessarily their livelihood. When churches regard evangelism as the very thing that keeps them alive, it becomes more than important; it becomes essential. Beautiful sanctuaries, well-organized kitchens, and the annual chili-feed are all important, but our survival as churches depends on our commitment to effectively fish for people.

When our church began, we had no building and no sign because we were meeting in rented space each weekend. We were not visible in the community so we had to rely on a variety of different marketing methods to get the word out about our church and to attract people to the weekend services. We used our entire tackle box to get the word out—marketing lists, phone calling campaigns, direct mail, newspaper ads, and word of mouth. Here are a few examples of our approach. As you read, think about your community and how you might apply one or more of these ideas to fish for people in your area.

Marketing Lists and Phone Calling Campaigns
Evangelism requires that you connect on a personal level with the people in your community. One way to do this is to conduct a phone calling campaign to speak to as many people as possible. We purchased a crisscross directory, which is a phone book arranged by street address, that helped us select potential people to contact in our area. Since we didn't have a church building at that point, we set up a phone bank in the basement of a sister church; and over the course of six evenings, callers made phone calls to the households from our list.

Using a script, the callers first asked the person if he or she was actively involved in a church. If the response was no, the caller would ask if we could send information about our new church. About six hundred of the six thousand households contacted responded that they were not involved in a local church and would be willing to receive additional information. This telemarketing method resulted in a database of six hundred households, totaling close to 1800 individuals who had identified themselves as either non religious or nominally religious, exactly who we were trying to reach! Of our charter households, almost all were first made aware of the church as a result of this initial phone calling outreach. Telemarketing is not always well received in today's society. However, if done properly and respectfully, it can be a very effective tool in your evangelism tackle box.

Once you've made an initial contact with those in your area, that doesn't mean that the research is over. You must continually analyze your surroundings. We continue to use marketing lists and research as a way of keeping informed about our community and as a way of identifying those we are trying to reach. For example, when apartment complexes began rising up all around our central campus, we acquired a marketing study that told us those living in the apartments would primarily be singles in their thirties. This research was a catalyst for us to launch a singles ministry eventually reaching thousands in the community. We purchased a mailing list targeted at singles within five miles of the church. We sent a direct-mail piece inviting them to the church, letting them know, that if they did not have a church family, we would love to be their church. We became very intentional when they arrived to speak language that would include them. We were careful to speak to everyone and avoid language that applied only to families or married couples. We also made certain we had great programming and ways for singles to connect quickly.

Those who fish know the value of research. They rely on reports provided by experts who analyze the local bodies of water and provide important information about the current fishing conditions, what species of fish are biting, where, and on what bait. Spending time analyzing this research aids the fisher in his or her quest for a productive day of fishing. What value do you see in adding market research to your evangelism tackle box?

Direct Marketing

Let's go back and spend a moment examining what happened immediately following the initial telemarketing campaign. We developed three direct-mail brochures aimed specifically at attracting the unchurched rather than luring members from other congregations. Each piece articulated our vision and included an invitation to the grand opening. Each brochure was mailed to approximately 10,000 households from a purchased marketing list. We also sent personalized letters and invitations to those who had indicated an interest in receiving information during the phone campaign.

Six weeks after the phone calling campaign, we held our first worship service. Of those in attendance, close to 120 were prospective members from the community. Almost all noted they heard about the church from the phone campaign or the direct mail piece. Over the next four years, while we worshiped in rented space, we relied heavily on direct mail to get the word out about the church. We also discovered that direct mail actually became more effective the longer we used it as many people would respond only after receiving our mailings for two or three years.

Adam offers this advice about direct mail,

> Do it well, do it positively, do it regularly, and send it to thousands of households. Doing it well means that the quality, the concept, the artwork, the paper, and the colors should all be sharp. A poorly designed mailer can do more harm than good. I suggest having the senior pastor and one or two talented graphic or marketing people design the piece. It should not be designed or tweaked by committee. The piece will lose its edge and effectiveness if too many people are a part of the process. Doing it positively means that your message should be a positive one; negative messages tend to turn unchurched people away (though the people in your church may like them). Doing it regularly means sending it out two to three times per year. Direct mailing has a residual effect; many respond only after the fourth or fifth, or sixth mailing they receive. Finally, direct mail works on the "law of large numbers." Your response rate for a well-designed direct mail piece might be only one-tenth of one percent; if you send out three thousand pieces that might indicate that as few as three to as many as ten households would visit. Often the response rate is much higher, but be prepared for a rate within this range. If the cost of your direct mail piece is two thousand to three thousand dollars, but three households join as a result, it would well pay for itself in the first year (*Leading Beyond the Walls*, page 36).

Direct mail is an important evangelism tool at Church Of the Resurrection. We send direct-mail pieces for special events such as the opening of new buildings on our campus, for the launch of new ministries such as young adults, support groups, and for special events such as a summer community fellowship event. We also send approximately three direct-mail pieces a year, most often in the form of a postcard, inviting people to worship. One is typically in August as families are finishing summer break and preparing to go back to school, and our two largest mailings are at Easter and Christmas when non and nominally religious people naturally consider going to church. These postcards offer a personal, compelling invitation to attend worship.

Another way we use direct marketing is to print extra copies of the direct mail postcards and place them in the weekend worship bulletins. We are very specific with our members, telling them that the postcards are not for them but are instead a tool for them to use to invite a friend. We ask members to pray for a friend, a co-worker, a neighbor who does not go to church, and then encourage them to hand deliver the postcard inviting this person to attend worship. The combination of the prayer, personal invitation, and the printed postcard is very persuasive in getting people to visit.

Candlelight Christmas Eve

Think about the high-attendance times of your church year. If you took a survey, most churches would probably say that Christmas and Easter are the most-attended services. Our growth at Church of the Resurrection has, in large part, been driven by our Candlelight Christmas Eve Worship Services. In fact, each year we find our Christmas Eve attendance will be a little more than double the average fall worship attendance. The worship services are designed so that when visitors come, they feel welcome and understand what is happening in the service. We offer the highest quality worship experience possible with great music and a sermon designed for new people who do not necessarily know Christ, helping them understand what Christmas really means. By offering multiple worship service times, we make sure that all those who attend for the first time on Christmas Eve will have a seat when they arrive.

This past Christmas Eve we offered two worship services on Christmas Eve "eve" at 6:00 and 8:00 pm, and then nine services on Christmas Eve. Each service was designed with a specific target in mind. For example, the Christmas Eve "eve" services were designed for those who enjoy contemporary music. On Christmas Eve, the 1:00 pm service was designed for senior adults and included an old-fashion Christmas sing-along. The 3:00 pm was designed for families with young children and included a shorter sermon and other worship elements designed specifically for children. The 5:00 pm service was geared to families with teenagers and had our student ministry band and youth choirs offering leadership in worship.

History tells us that a first-time visitor will most likely attend either the 7:00 or 9:00 pm service on Christmas Eve, so these services are more traditional with hymns they may have sung as a child or young person. Because we know these services will be the most heavily attended times, and because we want to ensure that all our visitors have a seat, we offer overflow worship in another location in the building. The overflow space is well-prepared for worship, including live worship leadership and the sermon via DVD or live feed. We ask our leaders and church members to worship in the overflow service leaving empty seats available for first-time visitors in the main sanctuary. Finally, the 11:00 pm service is designed to conclude at midnight (Christmas Day) with communion in addition to the powerful passing of the light.

Every year we receive e-mails from people who tell us that they gave their lives to Christ for the first time during a Candlelight Christmas Eve worship service. The image of Christ entering a broken world and piercing the darkness with light is brought to life in a transformational experience on Christmas Eve.

You may not have need for several service options, but it is very important to view the Christmas Eve service as an evangelism opportunity. Your sanctuary will be filled with members and their out-of-town guests as well as those in your community who may not know why they go to church on Christmas Eve, they just know they always do. Here is your chance to connect with them and open them up to the life-changing love of God that comes to us through Jesus Christ. Don't waste an opportunity to reach this group of people!

Fishing Expeditions

Since we have identified Christmas Eve and Easter as high-visitor-attendance services, we want to be intentional about not only communicating the love of God to these visitors, but also to connect them to our church. In order to inspire the holiday visitors to return to church, we announce a new series of sermons that starts right after the holiday. We make sure that these sermon series speak directly to the questions or concerns of unchurched persons. *We call these sermon series immediately following "fishing expeditions," drawing from Jesus' invitation to the disciples to become "fishers of people." Our aim is to cast out the net on Christmas Eve or Easter when the largest number of non and nominally religious people are present in worship, and try to encourage them to return for worship after the holiday (Unleashing the Word, page 63).* The fishing expeditions are specifically aimed at asking the question, "What would unchurched people want or need to hear in order to come back to the church?"

One young man with whom Adam spoke typifies many non-religious or nominally-religious people. John was 24 years old when Adam first met him. John's father told Adam that John had been turned off by religion and by Christianity in particular, and asked if Adam would be willing to meet with him. And so John came to Adam's office. Here was this brash young man, respectful, but very clear he was not a Christian, and there were very specific reasons why he wasn't. He then laid out the eight reasons why he was not a Christian. Adam listened. After John was finished, Adam shared some thoughts, but what Adam realized was that John was reacting to a certain picture of Christianity that was not Adam's picture of Christianity. In fact, what John had laid out was what many people think about the gospel and the Christian faith. John had just come back from the military. He'd been in the service for six years and was on the initial invading force going into Iraq. During that time, he had watched several of his friends killed. John wanted to know if there was a loving God, then why hadn't his friends been spared? What John was asking is the number one question non-religious people ask and what they tell us is the largest reason they're not followers of Jesus Christ: "Why do bad things happen to good people?" So Adam preached a fishing expedition sermon series following that interview called "Conversations with an Atheist."

Have you thought about how you could follow up a Christmas Eve worship service with an invitation to join you for a sermon series aimed at answering questions a non or nominally religious person might be asking? Imagine what would happen if you announce on Christmas Eve, "Starting next week, I'm going to be preaching a series asking the question, "Why do bad things happen to good people? You've wrestled with prayers that weren't answered. You've seen things happen that you just couldn't reconcile with a good and loving God. If you ever wrestle with these questions, I'd like to invite you to come back for our next three sermons on Where Was God When: The Problem of Evil and the Providence of God." Now, you announce that series of sermons on Christmas Eve and I guarantee you, your members are all going to want to come and hear what you have to say. But, the non-religious and nominally-religious people like John, are going to want to come to hear what you have to say in answer to this question as well.

Newspaper and Radio Advertising
Although we have determined direct mail is one of our most successful forms of promotion to attract first-time visitors, there are other methods of paid marketing. One is newspaper advertising. We advertise each week in the Faith section of the Kansas City *Star* as well as in several community papers. When you think about it, though, most non and nominally religious people will most likely not be reading the Faith section of your local newspaper. Who reads the Faith section? Yes, churched people for the most part. We have been very clear since the beginning of our church, that it is not our intent to attract people who are already attending another church in the area. So why would we advertise here? We keep this weekly ad in the paper because we find that people who are moving into the area or who are visiting the area will look here as a source to find a local church to visit.

You can also take advantage of your local community event calendars. Most of these are free, so we post the dates for programs we feel would be attractive to the community such as parenting classes, singles dances, or a special guest speaker. Stories written about church members or features about your church can also attract visitors to your church. Each fall we host a 5K walk/run called Sacred Steps. The proceeds from the event fund ground-level projects in Sub-Saharan Africa to overcome the devastation caused by

HIV/AIDS. Before one of these runs, a young woman read the story about our event. She did not attend church, but she loved to run so she made a decision to participate. She became so excited about the mission that she became the largest fund-raiser and has since become active in the church. We have had articles written about our neighborhood food drives, our Christmas Eve services, and our work with the inner city schools, among others.

We have also started purchasing advertising space on a local secular radio station for several weeks prior to Christmas and Easter. We create 60-second spots aimed at teaching a parable that might connect with an everyday life question or experience. Here is a sample script from one of the spots this past Christmas:

The Gift on Behalf of Others

Are you looking for some last minute gift ideas? Can't decide what to give someone who has everything?

Hi, I'm Adam Hamilton, Senior Pastor of the Church of the Resurrection.

A friend recently gave me a great Christmas gift—a share of a sheep that was donated to a family in a third world country. I recently gave a gift to a friend of ten meals provided in his honor to those who are homeless in a shelter here in Kansas City.

If you're looking for a great gift to give someone who has everything, consider giving a gift in their honor to someone who has nothing. A gift of $10, $20 or $50 to area agencies that work with low income people can make a difference and be a great way to let your friends and family know that you care about them, and you care about others.

If you'd like help finding a way to give this kind of gift, check out our Web site at www.cor.org where you can find links to area agencies and suggestions and opportunities for how you can work directly with them to give gifts that really will make a difference. And, if you don't yet have plans to attend a Christmas Eve Candlelight service, I'd like to invite you to join us for one hour—one hour that will help you remember what Christmas is really all about.

Consider this for a moment: unchurched people will only visit a church of which they have some awareness. If they are not aware of your church, how can they find you? Particularly during Christmas and Easter when a non or nominally religious person might be motivated to attend worship, it is important to have a strong marketing presence out in your community.

As any good fisher knows, you may not always catch a fish in your favorite fishing hole each time you visit, but if you are persistent, you will eventually reel one in. Although newspaper and radio may not be the most effective forms of attracting visitors, they give you alternative methods of "bait." Some marketers will tell you it takes seven approaches to get a message across to a "customer," and these are two good approaches to keep the message about your church visible in the community.

Web site

The Web is becoming an increasingly important tool for evangelism. If you have sent out direct-mail pieces and placed radio and newspaper advertisements telling people about your church, they will more than likely look on your Web site before they decide whether to "bite." For many it will be their first visit to your church. Knowing this guides our commitment to organizing information on the homepage with a first-time visitor in mind. There is a specific place on our home page for visitors to sign up for a weekly e-newsletter. Because these e-newsletters have links embedded in the articles, we have found it is our primary driver back to our site for not only our members, but visitors as well.

Your home page should be designed with an easy navigation system and be tied to your vision, purpose, and mission. Visitors should be able to easily read more about your church, find worship times, see the calendar of the featured events, and find directions. We like to post a video about the upcoming sermon series and offer videos for people watch the past week's sermon. Consistency throughout the site will make it easy to move between pages where a visitor can view, read about, and register for any event online. In addition, you want to make it easy to find out how to contact someone for additional information or to ask a general question.

What does your Web site communicate about your church? Does the Web site make your visitors feel welcome? Is it easy to navigate? Or, is it full of outdated information that sends people away in confusion and frustration?

Social Media

Andrew Conard, Internet Campus Pastor at Church of the Resurrection says, "Churches are using Facebook in many ways to connect with congregants and those who are outside the congregation. Facebook is an online space in which people connect with each other and engage in the lives of friends and family. As the church, we are called to be where people are, and Facebook and other online communities are places where people today interact."

Consider setting up a page that provides basic information about worship time, updates on events, and opportunities to engage with others. Some of this information could also exist on a Web site, but Facebook provides a free avenue for connection and allows for greater interactivity. Having a presence on Facebook can facilitate connections between church members and make it easier for current attendees to invite their friends.

Twitter provides a service in which persons or organizations respond to the question, "What are you doing?" in 140 characters or less. Churches can use Twitter to provide updates, called "tweets," on what is happening in the church and opportunities to be involved. Because it is possible to "retweet" a message, spreading a received message to a group of followers, Twitter can become a tool for evangelism. Churches can provide updates that can be spread through circles of influence to communicate good news.

Community Events

We recognize that our building itself is bait that lures people to our church. For some, their first experience of the church may be participating in a community blood drive, college graduation, symphony concert, Boy Scout meeting, homeowners association meeting, or other community event. Because we recognize our building is an important evangelism tool, we have been intentional about opening our doors to the community and allowing it to be used for outside events. We make sure each person who comes to our campus feels welcomed and comfortable. More on how we do that in the next chapter. Weddings and funerals also provide an incredible opportunity for evangelism. During a wedding you have the opportunity to reach people for Christ and help give spiritual direction for a family and for generations to come.

> We have hundreds of people who have joined our church who indicate that the first time they ever visited was at one of our weddings. A wedding done well, not only blesses the bride and groom, but is an opportunity to reach guests who may not have been in church in years. Likewise, a wedding done poorly, will reinforce for these same people all the reasons they do not attend church (*Leading Beyond the Walls,* pages 117- 118).

As is the case with weddings, we have had hundreds of people who first began attending Church of the Resurrection at a funeral and who eventually became members. Every funeral is filled with a large number of people who may not darken the door of a church at any other time. And they are wrestling with truly important questions about death, the meaning and purpose of life, how we understand God's love in relationship to evil and suffering, and so much more. A well-led funeral can move persons to want to reconnect with God and to visit your church. The key is in spending time with the family and then taking the time to develop a quality, meaningful ministry experience at the funeral (*Leading Beyond the Walls*, page 124).

Word of Mouth

Direct marketing, newspaper, radio, Web site are all important tools for attracting visitors, but often the most effective evangelism method is personal invitation. Evangelism happens best by relationships, when one person who gets excited about his or her faith invites another person along for the journey. Research has shown that unchurched people are more likely to visit a church if someone they know, like a neighbor, close friend, co-worker, or family member, invites them. Over 90 percent of those who attend our membership coffee tell us they visited because someone invited them. So, we have found ways to provide tools to our church members so they can effectively "fish for people" in a way that they feel comfortable.

Our hope is that these tools help break down barriers of intimidation and fear in reaching out. For example, for each of our sermon series, including the fishing expeditions, we print extra sermon postcards and insert them into the weekly worship bulletins. Adam intentionally tells the congregation that the postcards are not for them, but instead to be used as an invitation. In addition to the postcards, we have found technology to be a useful tool. We have developed an e-vite for each of our series. It is a link on our Web site that church members can go to, type in the e-mail addresses for those they would like to invite, and write a personal message of invitation. The e-mail is sent with the personal message and a link to a video promotion about the upcoming series and invitation to church.

We also keep a full supply of pocket testaments available for our members. Adam encourages them to find a few extra minutes wherever they are and open it up and start reading. He challenges them to get caught reading their Bibles and then give it away. Give the pocket testament away! Just like the sermon postcards, he reminds the congregation that the pocket testaments are not for them, but instead to be given away.

These tools are a few nonthreatening ways for our members to invite friends, family, and neighbors to church, and for them to feel more confident in the process. Finally, what we have discovered is that preaching is the most effective bait that attracts visitors back to worship. All the other tactics may get visitors in the doors, but the sermon is the thing that will bring people back. Our senior pastor's goal is to preach sermons that share the Good News and invite people to respond. He has been quoted as saying "my job is to be the tastiest worm possible."

Evangelism is helping people hear the good news of the gospel and motivating them to respond. Marketing, as it relates to the church then, is the effort made to persuade others of their need for Jesus Christ, while explaining the ways your church can help meet this need, and doing so in a way that inspires, motivates, and invites them to respond.

How good do you think your congregation is at attracting and inviting people to come to church? How are you inspiring and helping your congregation members to invite their friends? Are you intentional about reaching out to unchurched people in your community and finding ways to attract and persuade them to come in?

Chapter Three
Transforming to a Welcoming Environment

Offer hospitality to one another without grumbling. —1 Peter 4:9

Each year my family spends a week during the winter in Destin, Florida. For a Midwesterner, time in the Florida sun during the winter is a treasured experience. One of the favorite activities for my husband and son is to fish from one of the local jetties with my stepfather and brother-in-law. They love getting up early in the morning, packing lunches and snacks, making a day of it. We look forward to enjoying their prize catch of grouper, red fish, and trigger fish. This past winter, my brother-in-law and stepfather decided to catch grouper by using shrimp as bait.

They settled in on the jetty, baiting their hooks with the shrimp. Within seconds my brother-in-law's pole dipped deep into the water signaling the bite of a fish, and then his second pole dipped. Wow, what excitement! He spent the next few hours attracting and reeling in fish after fish. My stepfather on the other hand was not getting a bite. What was going on? They were fishing in the same location, and with the same bait. Finally, in exasperation, my stepfather asked my brother-in-law what he was doing to attract so many fish. He discovered that my brother-in-law had taken an extra step in preparing his bait. My stepfather had been putting the shrimp from his bait bucket right on to the hook, while my brother-in-law had taken the time to carefully peel each shrimp, making it more inviting to the fish. He had taken an extra step in order to most effectively attract the fish to the waiting hook.

Growing churches understand that to attract first-time visitors, you have to pay attention to detail and do the extra things. Attention to the little things matters to a first-time visitor. According to research, visitors will decide in three to eight minutes whether they'll return. Dynamic and growing churches recognize that little things play a key role in their success or failure. First-time visitors may form a negative impression of the kind of church you are, and may never have an opportunity to see your strengths if you have not paid attention to the little things. A first-time visitor begins formulating feelings about your congregation before getting out of the car. These impressions are formed by the appearance of your facilities and grounds, the quality of your signage, the congestion in your parking lot, the friendliness of the congregation, the cleanliness of your nursery, and other factors.

Having considered marketing strategies to invite people into church, your task now is to pay attention to the details so that your building, people, and programs work together to create a positive first impression. Every time a first-time visitor walks in the doors of your church, an opportunity unfolds. This individual has taken the time to worship with you for some reason. We look at every first-time visitor as someone who may be genuinely unchurched, for whom this may be their first time in years that he or she has visited a church. It may have taken a great deal of courage, or a great need that prompted him or her to come. Often visitors come only after a friend has invited them five or six times, or after having received one of our mailings seven times. If this is the case, we want to do everything in our power to help the visitor feel the welcome of Christ through the church and to motivate him or her to return the following week.

Recently we had the members of our trustees tour our facilities with the eye of a first-time visitor. They each had a digital camera and were asked to take a picture of anything they saw that would not be attractive to visitors. They discovered poor directional signage, peeling paint, stained carpet and ceiling tiles, potholes in the parking lot, unsightly landscaping, and nurseries that were difficult to access. These pictures were used to create action steps for correction, and over the next year we addressed each issue. When was the last time you took a look at your building and programs from the perspective of a first-time visitor? Let's look at some components of transforming your church into a welcoming environment.

Signage
When visitors approach your building, do they know where to go? It can be

hard to imagine their perspective if you've been in church all of your life, but take a minute to see with a visitor's eyes. Do you know where to park? Do you know which entrance to walk in? Do you know where to go once you're in? Appropriate signage puts visitors at ease and points them exactly where they need to go. It is also an indicator that you are expecting visitors and that you have prepared for their arrival.

Interior signage should direct people to specific locations such as the nearest restroom, information area, classrooms, nurseries, check-in locations, and the sanctuary. All signage should be visible and easy to read. In 1996, we moved into a beautiful children's education space. We had intentionally spent time making sure each room was clearly labeled so families would know where to take their children. However, we hadn't considered that when the hallways were filled with people during check-in, the signs would not be visible. We had beautiful signage, but it was flat on the wall at shoulder level and was covered up by the crowds of people gathering in the hallway. We spent the next month ordering and redoing the signage for this building with new signs perpendicular to the wall and above the doorway, clearly visible to all. If you ever visit this building, you will see the signs flat against the wall at shoulder level, and signs above the door. Now you'll know the story as to why there are two signs in this hallway. Attention to the little things is important.

Have you ever entered a church, where the doors or walls are cluttered with left over tape from old signs or covered with signs with information about different meetings or events? What did this look like to you? What did it communicate? It is not attractive, and in many ways communicates that you had not thought through all the details of getting information out to people and may not be prepared. To avoid this, we have a policy against handmade signs and taping signs to the walls and doors. We keep specially purchased floor sign holders that we use to communicate a room change or meeting information. We print the information on a standard piece of copy paper and insert it into the sign holder to get a professional and polished look.

We have special signs for outdoor use, directing people where to park during community events, wedding, funerals, and conferences. The main campus outdoor signage is not always effective in giving specific information about the location of special events. In order to welcome those who might be coming to the church for something besides worship, these portable signs are used to welcome them and to provide direction on where to park so they are at the closest entrance to the building where the event is being held. These signs are inexpensive and can be purchased from most any printing or office supply store. They are weatherproof and on metal stands that are easily placed in the ground. Again, this is just another way to let visitors know that you planned for their arrival.

Visitor Parking

A few years ago, my family and I visited a large church in Dallas, Texas. We had read a lot about this church and were excited for our first visit. When we arrived, the parking lot was extremely congested and we discovered three large buildings. There were large numbers of people entering each of the buildings, and with no outdoor signage marking the buildings, we were not able to tell which of the buildings was the main worship center. After circling the full parking lot several times we finally found a parking spot toward the back of one of the lots. We entered the building closest to where we had parked, only to discover it was the children's building. This was a secure area so we had two options. One, we would need to go back outside and around the building to the main sanctuary, or we could use the outer hallways inside the building to wind our way around until we came to the main foyer. We decided to go outside, finally arriving at the main sanctuary, only to discover that the doors to the worship center were closed because the worship service had started. After the opening welcome, prayer, and songs, we were allowed in, but to be honest, I was embarrassed to go in late, and felt unsettled, anxious, and like an outsider.

To welcome visitors from the minute they pull into the parking lot, you need to have a special parking area reserved for them. By having this special area, you can strategically assign parking lot greeters to welcome them and facilitate which entrances most first-time visitors will enter. When you know that your greeters are directing all visitors through a particular entrance, you know where to set up a special information station that you know they'll find. As visitors enter our parking lot, the outdoor signage invites a first-time visitor to turn on their hazard lights. By doing this, the parking lot greeters know to direct them to the lot we have reserved especially for them. This lot is located

close to the building with quick and easy access into the main building.
We have discovered that many of our first-time visitors are the last to arrive
for worship, so having parking spaces just for them that are closest to the
building gives them easy access and helps them to get in quicker with less
anxiety and stress. Our ushers and greeters are also trained to be on the lookout
for visitors and assist them quickly if needed. The only time we do not allow
entrance into our sanctuary is 30 to 45 minutes prior to worship during the
technical run and for a brief 30 seconds during the opening prayer. However,
if a visitor walks in during one of these times, our ushers greet them warmly
and help them find a seat. Again, it is a little detail that demonstrates you are
expecting them, and that they are welcomed.

Parking Lot Attendants

One of the first personal touches our visitors receive is from our parking lot
greeter ministry. This team serves several purposes. They greet our first-time
visitors in the specially designated area and answer any initial questions.
Second, they keep the traffic moving so that people enter the parking lots
quickly, efficiently, and safely. Just trying to find a place to park can be
stressful for many, and this team helps eliminate this stress by keeping the
traffic flowing smoothly.

When we first launched the idea of this ministry, many thought, "Who will
sign up to stand in the parking lot in the rain, snow, chilling cold of winter, and
brutal heat of summer?" Our senior pastor cast a compelling vision about the
importance of this ministry, calling people to be a part of the front line of
welcoming our visitors and caring for our congregation. This is now one of our
strongest and most dedicated teams. They arrive early to serve each week no
matter the weather. They begin by checking to make sure the parking lots are
free of trash and clutter because little things matter. They gather as a team for
prayer and then they stand in their assigned parking lot smiling, waving,
directing traffic, and providing care for all who arrive.

Greeters

Another element of making a good first impression is caring greeters at every
entrance to the building. These greeters give a warm welcome to all who enter,
and their enthusiasm for the church sets the tone and makes a difference. Their

purpose is to reflect the love of Christ by being welcoming, hospitable, and gracious to all who enter our church home. They wear specially marked greeter nametags clearly identifying who they are. They help provide direction not by pointing the way but by personally taking a visitor to the location he or she is looking for. They are attentive to people who may need assistance, such as the elderly or a family with infants and young children.

Our greeters receive a very high level of training that includes how to be friendly, without being overly friendly. The goal is to welcome people, without overwhelming them. Greeters are trained to reach out their hand to offer a welcoming handshake, and to say "Welcome to Church of the Resurrection. We are so glad you are here." They are also trained to welcome the children, not just the adults. One family shared that the turning point of their decision to join the church was when they entered; the greeter not only greeted them, but bent down and greeted their children. To this visiting family, it was a sign that this was a church that valued and welcomed children. Visitors notice little things!

Because greeters are in the main gathering places in your church, it can be easy for their friends to come up to them and begin talking. It's a natural thing that friends want to catch up on Sunday mornings. However, when visitors see others huddled in conversations, they can feel like they don't belong. The goal is for them to feel comfortable and not like an outsider from the very beginning, so pay attention to any barriers to creating this environment and eliminate them. We have been intentional in training our greeters that when a friend approaches while they are greeting and begins to go into a deeper conversation to say, "I am serving right now and will be finished in 15 minutes. I can't wait to hear more. Let's meet after service to catch up." You want to make sure that your visitors don't feel like outsiders the minute they walk in the door.

Nametags

Do you remember the old sitcom Cheers—a local bar where people gathered for friendship, fellowship, and to talk about life? I'm sure you remember the theme song about finding a place "where everybody knows your name." People gather each week in church to find friendship, to discuss life, and to experience fellowship with others. To remove an immediate barrier of the pressure to remember names, we have nametags printed for all of our members, volunteers, and staff. We even invite our regular visitors to get a nametag if they so desire. It is one way for us to call each other by name, making our connections more personal. Staff and lead volunteer nametags also provide a quick way for visitors to know who to contact if needed. We place bulk orders of clip-on nametags with our church name preprinted. Using clear labels and a label machine, we are able to quickly make a personalized nametag for anyone who requests one. We encourage our members and staff to wear their nametags to all church events and gatherings. Being able to greet someone by name is the first step to relationship building and is a great bridge to creating a culture of friendliness.

Clean Facilities

Visitor friendly churches pay attention to details, especially when it comes to the overall cleanliness and appearance of your facility. This past winter, we had a group of people enjoying a bonfire complete with hot chocolate and s'mores. I couldn't wait to get a nice cup of the hot chocolate. It looked delicious with its rich, dark chocolate color. As I poured my first cup and took a big drink, I was stunned. The hot chocolate was not hot; it was cold. I put down my cup in disappointment. It was just a little thing, but it ruined the experience because someone failed to pay attention to one small detail: to keep the hot chocolate heated while it was being served.

I wonder what little things in our churches ruin the experience for people. Some time ago Adam went to visit a church building. A senior pastor had invited him and asked him to pretend to be a first-time visitor, to see everything through the eyes of a first-time visitor and to provide some critique and suggestions. When Adam drove into the parking lot, the first thing he noticed was that dogs had gotten into the trash that had been placed outside and trash was spread all over the church grounds. He also noticed that the grass had not been mowed. That began to tell a story about the church.

When Adam went inside, the church foyer was cluttered with mission donations, and the reception desk was covered with old papers, out-of-date brochures, and lost and found articles. The pastor first wanted to show Adam the sanctuary, but Adam said, "Don't show me your sanctuary; I want to see your nursery." The pastor was perplexed but took Adam to his nursery area. Adam explained to the pastor that while doing some research before coming, he had discovered that there were many families with small children in the neighborhood where the church was located. In order to reach the unchurched families in this area, an excellent program for young children would be key.

As they walked into the nursery, Adam began to look around. He could smell the ripe and distinguished fragrance of dirty diapers and mildew, masked with a faint scent of Lysol. The ceiling tiles in the nursery and children's classrooms were stained, toys were broken, and the rooms were poorly lit. Adam told the pastor, "I don't need to see anything else about your building, because if I were a first-time visitor with a small child, I wouldn't feel safe leaving my child in your nursery and I would not be back."

Growing, dynamic churches are constantly looking around to see what could be done a little better. We have made major strides in keeping our narthex free of clutter by designating spaces for mission collection, lost and found, coat storage, and so forth. We have set times throughout the day where the bathrooms are cleaned and restocked and trash is picked up. We do touchup paint regularly and have a regular cycle for replacing stained ceiling tiles. We also ask that our mowing crews come in on Friday of each week so that our grass looks well-kept and manicured for our weekend guests. We do a lot of this by enlisting the help of volunteer work teams. We don't always get it perfect, but we are constantly asking the questions: What can we do better to create a welcoming space for visitors? Does the condition of our facility honor God? Does it say that we believe what we are doing here is important? Does it demonstrate quality and caring?

Visitor-Friendly Worship Service

If your efforts to attract visitors to your church are successful through your marketing and getting the little things right, you will find your worship services each week filled with first-time visitors. Your teams will have welcomed visitors from the parking lot to the foyer, creating an environment where they feel like they belong. You will have transformed your space into a welcoming place where no one is feels like an outsider.

Your worship service should reflect the same welcoming concepts. Worship should be the place where visitors feel the most like they belong, but for many, it is the place where they feel the most on the outside. I have been spending time in Eurasia facilitating leadership development seminars and working with church leaders. During the worship services, I find myself confused as to when I am to stand, sit, pray, sing, or simply listen. This is in part because I don't understand the language, but it is not that far of a stretch as an analogy for the way a visitor may feel in your church. You want to go out of your way to make sure visitors know what's going on during worship and not assume that they will know your cues.

Our aim is to offer worship that is for our congregation, a blend of Scripture, tradition, experience, and reason. We don't want to sacrifice our identity for the sake of not confusing newcomers. Rather, we want to help them understand what we do in worship and why we do it. The key to helping first-time visitors fully engage in worship is to interpret, explain, and adequately set up each element so that they can understand that in which they are invited to participate. Here are a few ideas of how we attempt to make sure our first-time visitors are engaged and not left feeling like they are on the outside.

Welcoming Announcement

When it comes to the beginning of worship, whoever speaks first sets the emotional and spiritual tone of the service. We always have a high-energy person deliver the welcome. If you don't want a low-energy service, do not have a low-energy person give the words of welcome. We begin worship each week with these words, "Welcome to the United Methodist Church of the Resurrection! We are so excited that you are here today! My name is Adam Hamilton; I am the senior pastor and we are so grateful that you have chosen to worship with us today!" The introduction of the worship leader or pastor by name is important. When your pastor or worship leader does not introduce him or herself and proceeds to lead worship, a first-time visitor wonders, "Who is this person?" Can you imagine inviting a visitor into your home, and not introducing yourself? This is one small way to welcome visitors—tell them who you are before you lead your part of worship.

Greeting Time

In several churches I have visited, I've been given a special nametag to wear because I am a visitor, or I am asked to stand at a certain point in the service to be recognized. At our church, we are careful not to make our visitors stand out. We do not give them special visitor nametags or make them stand up to be recognized. Most visitors do not wish to be recognized or called out, but they do want to feel like someone noticed that they were there—they want others to be friendly and welcoming. Immediately following the words of welcome during worship, we invite the members of the congregation to stand and greet one another. Our worship leader will say, "Let's take a moment to welcome one another. Sitting around you may be people who are visitors. There may be someone sitting next to you who had a very difficult week and just needs to feel the warmth and encouragement of another. With that in mind, let's welcome one another. Will you welcome those around you by introducing yourself by name?" The energy level in the room goes up immediately and hopefully, members are mindful of the need others may have for a brief welcome. At times, we will invite people to tell those around them how long they have been coming to the church, or where their hometown is, or some other bit of information that encourages a sense of connection and sharing. This helps to build community and helps visitors find a connection point before worship begins.

Attendance Notebooks and Information for Visitors

After the opening hymns and prayer of confession, we pass an attendance notebook down each row to capture attendance. The pastor will say, "I invite our ushers to come forward and hand out our attendance notebooks. If you would, please sign in and let us know that you are here. As you are signing in, take a look to see who is sitting next to you and welcome those persons by name after this service of worship. If you are a visitor, the information on the left hand side is there for you to take so please help yourself. Once the book is at the end of the aisle, please pass it back to the beginning of the aisle so the folks on the other side can see who you are."

The left hand side of the notebook includes our most recent newsletter, current sermon series postcard, and a flyer about the church. After each worship service, volunteers restock each folder so the information is available for visitors at the next service. The visitors quickly recognize this as one more example that we were waiting and prepared for their visit.

Explaining each Worship Element

We don't assume visitors understand the transitions between the opening hymns, prayers of confession, baptisms, Scripture readings, sermon, or offering. We want our visitors to feel welcomed at each point in the worship service.

At the beginning of worship, we offer words of instruction to help set expectations for what will happen in the service. The welcoming pastor says, "We have gathered here to worship God, to sing praise to God's name, to lift up our prayers for thanksgiving and confession. We've come to lay before God our concerns. Our hope is that God will speak to you through the music, the reading of Scripture, and the message, that we might know God's will for our lives. We hope you will leave renewed and refreshed and ready to serve God in the world. With that in mind, let's take a moment to pray." Then during the opening prayer, the pastor may invite them to lay their hands on their lap, open palmed, and to repeat a prayer line by line like, "Lord, help me to set aside all the thoughts that compete with you for my attention. Help me to worship you with my lips and with my heart." Or, we may simply pray a similar prayer on their behalf and then with enthusiasm the pastor will say, "Let's stand together and worship the Lord."

We project the words to the songs, the Lord's Prayer and any special reading or liturgy on our screens, or we print them in the bulletin. We don't assume people know the words to any of the liturgies, prayers, praise songs, or hymns. When we participate in the sacraments, our pastors give words of instruction as a way of helping all feel included.

Connection Point

The Connection Point is located in our main narthex or foyer. It is our central location for high level customer service. Trained volunteers serve at the Connection Point with direct access to the church computer system, allowing them to access information, register people for programs or events, answer questions, provide directions or pass along a ministry flyer, and send e-mails to ministry connectors for follow-up. We also keep visitor packets at the Connection Point. Visitor packets contain ministry flyers, a letter from our senior pastor, a DVD of a sermon, and a map of our campus.

Coffee and Refreshments for Fellowship

After we have set up an environment of welcome from our parking lot to the sanctuary, we maintain this same sense of welcome by keeping coffee and tea stations located throughout our narthex area. Coffee and refreshments create a sense of fellowship and hospitality. It encourages people to linger after worship to visit and connect with others. Even before we had our coffee café, we used rolling utility carts with 60-cup coffee pots or catered in coffee from a local grocery store.

Making Room for Visitors

From the beginning, we've made having open seats available for visitors a high priority. Our ushers are trained to be attentive as they look for visitors. We have discovered something about visitors: most often, they arrive last to the sanctuary. And, if your congregation is like ours, your members seem to sit toward the back and on the aisle leaving the middle sections of each row open. So, where do visitors get to sit if they arrive late? That's right, in the front—after they have crawled over the people sitting on the aisle to get to their seats! We do a few things to be proactive to help avoid this situation for our visitors. First, we ask that the ushers are constantly surveying the room for open seats so that when visitors arrive, they can quickly assist them to their seat. Second, the worship leader at the beginning of worship will invite people to move to the middle, making room for those who may arrive late.

Let's also briefly consider how many people your building can hold. Let's say your sanctuary seats one hundred fifty people. You already know that the true capacity of the room is not really one hundred fifty. It will do from time to time, but if this room is filled and every seat taken every Sunday, eventually, the attendance will drop by about twenty to thirty. When a room is overcrowded, visitors begin to think, "Well, that was fun once, but I don't think I want to go back again. It was just too crowded."

You will also discover that when a room is overcrowded, people stop inviting their friends. So, as a general rule, you are full at 80 percent capacity. If you can seat one hundred fifty people, you are really full at one hundred twenty.

Think about how you can increase your capacity to welcome new people. You may add capacity through additional services or a new building project. Most times, it has to do with making the best use of the facility you have to create room for people when they are interested in coming.

Caring for Children

Your children's ministry may be one of the most important "hooks" in your tackle box when it comes to connecting people to your church. When our church was beginning, we were attracting a large number of families with children. During that time, I was serving as our children's ministry director and I would jokingly say, "Adam is the bait that brings them in, but our ministry to children is the hook that keeps them." Although that was said in jest, there is some truth to that statement. Parents will only leave their children where they feel each child is safe, and in our age of consumerism, where they believe their child is "having fun." We made it a priority to develop a ministry to children that was engaging, interactive, safe, family-centered, and yes, fun, all while guiding children on their journey to know, love, and serve God.

The safety of our children is one of our highest priorities. Our check-in and check out procedures ensure that a child passes only from our care into the care of his or her parents. Some churches have nursery check-in procedures, but nothing for the children's Sunday school classes. I would challenge you to think from a visitor's point of view about this, no matter your church size. If you have young children and leave them in the care of strangers, loving as they may be, for an hour, wouldn't you feel so much more at ease if the church had a procedure in place to ensure that your child would only be released from that classroom into your care? This is part of creating a welcoming environment for your visitors.

We have also been intentional about creating an environment for children that is engaging, using bright colors, age appropriate toys and activities, and interactive experiences. You want children to enter the space and say, "Wow!"

like they do when they arrive at their favorite pizza place or theme park. Creating a "wow" space does not have to be expensive. Enlist creative volunteers who will get excited about using their gifts and talents to help you evaluate your space. You will be surprised at the difference of simply changing the paint color from church taupe to something brighter and more vivid.

It is not only about paint choices and great toys, however. Those who serve with the children as greeters, Sunday school teachers, and leaders are very important to the first impression a visiting family receieves. Help your volunteers understand the important role they play in attracting and connecting children and their parents to your church. Their energy, their level of engagement with each child, and their love for the children will make a huge difference.

We have repeatedly found that as the children connect with their leaders and the other children in their classrooms, it is the children who are getting their parents out of bed for church on Sundays. They absolutely do not want to miss! Your pastor may spend many hours preparing excellent sermons, your parking lot team may have done an incredible job of welcoming people as they arrive, but if parents are not satisfied with the experience their children have, many simply will not return.

Receptionist and Voice Mail

One final note about transforming to a welcoming environment is to remember that some impressions may not be made in person. Make sure your phone receptionist is one of your most highly trained team members when it comes to customer service. Our receptionists are responsible for the highest level of customer service. Each staff member is required to keep our receptionists informed about current programs and ministry, plus any new opportunities. In addition, they stay up-to-date with the staff schedules so that they can best direct incoming calls. When the receptionist is not able to answer the phone directly, your voice-mail system serves as your information system. Arrange your voice-mail so that the incoming caller is able to get pertinent information first, and then provide the menu for additional options. We include our worship times and the list of our staff extensions as the first options available.

In addition, the emergency telephone number is provided, directing anyone with an urgent need to this number immediately.

Positive first impressions are an important hook in attracting first-time visitors to consider a second visit. Little things matter. Have you taken time to discover the little things that need attention at your church?

Chapter Four
Connection and Follow-up

Share with the God's people who are in need. Practice hospitality.
—Romans 12:13

This past winter I was in Russia doing leadership training for pastors and lay members. The subject of fishing came up in a casual conversation. A pastor asked me, "Do Americans really make fishing a sport where you catch fish and then release them?" I was a little surprised by his question because I had never really given much thought to this aspect of the sport—where the fisherman works hard at attracting the fish using all the right bait, just to release the catch. When I told him that was actually true, he responded, "Why would a fisherman work so hard to catch something and then just let it get away? When we fish, we go with the intention of keeping the fish."

His comments made me wonder a little bit about our churches. In what ways do we attract new visitors to the church but, without effective connection and follow-up strategies, let them get away? We have explored marketing strategies to attract visitors to your church. We have talked about the importance of paying attention to details and transforming into an environment that welcomes visitors and creates positive first impressions. But what about follow-up? Growing churches have effective follow-up and connection strategies.

At some point during the year, most every church will have a first-time visitor. Every time a first-time visitor walks through the doors of your church an opportunity unfolds. The question is: what kind of follow-up will you do to encourage that visitor to come back? What will you do to help him or her experience the welcome of Christ through your church and motivate that visitor to return the following week?

I recently joined a health club for the very first time. I had received numerous postcards and information in the mail for more than a year from this particular fitness center. I drive past it every day on my way to and from the church office and see the building and sign, and I overhear my co-workers talking about how much they enjoy working out at this center. Finally, I got the courage to try it out. Going for the first time was a real effort for me. I felt intimidated as I didn't know what to expect. I didn't know how to use the equipment, and I was concerned everyone working out would be much more advanced than I. I would be the outsider. Mustering all the courage I had, I walked through the door. I was greeted by a friendly trainer who acquainted me with the machines and helped me get started. I had a good experience on my first visit and had great intentions of returning. I know that working out is something that I need and is important for me to do, but that was over two months ago and I have yet to return. And, no one at the health center seems to have missed me, as I have not received any follow-up from them asking me when my next visit might be. So, each day when I drive by the facility on my way to work, I think, I really should get back, and I keep driving. Adam, in his book *Leading Beyond the Walls,* shares a similar story and goes on to say that this is where many of our first-time visitors find themselves after they visit our church. They have a great experience and believe attending church is important, but for some reason they lack the motivation to return.

Effective follow-up offers encouragement and motivation for the visitor to choose to return for a second, third, or fourth visit. This is among the most important things you will do if you are serious about reaching the unchurched in your community.

Mugging

Let's talk about what happens when someone visits our church for the first time. Remember from the last chapter that during the worship service we take time to find out who is visiting. During the service, while the special music is being performed, we invite the ushers to hand every row of people an attendance notebook. Our pastor says to the congregation, "If you would please sign in and let us know that you are here, we would be most grateful. As you are signing in, take a look to see who is sitting next to you and welcome those persons by name after this service of worship. If you are a first-time visitor, the information on the left hand side is there for you to take, so please help yourself. Once the notebook is at the end of the aisle, please pass it back to the beginning of the aisle so the folks on the other side can see who you are."

Now some people don't want to sign in and give you their name and address. However, when the pastor makes a point to invite them to sign in and furthermore has told the person sitting next to them to look and see who they are and to welcome them by name, it becomes more of a challenge. The person sitting next to you is going to know whether you signed in because he or she is going to try to "welcome you by name." We don't want to make this a high pressure situation, but the information in those notebooks informs how we connect and follow-up with visitors and members. After several years of being intentional about sign in, we have discovered that most will decide that they don't want to break the rules and happily sign in.

After each worship service, the attendance notebooks are collected. We have a team of volunteers who input the weekend attendance information so that we know exactly who was in worship and who was absent. If one of our members misses five weeks in a row, one of our volunteers contacts him or her personally. We want our members to know that they are missed. Taking attendance is time-consuming, but it is very important to the effective care of your congregation.

Not only do the attendance notepads help us keep up with our members, they also let us know who is visiting for the first time. The attendance notebooks have two forms to collect information. One form collects information for members and the other does so for visitors. By having these two forms, we are able to prioritize data entry. After the notebooks are collected following each service, visitor information is given to an onsite volunteer data entry team that immediately inputs the data into our system. After the information is entered, we use online mapping tools to print out detailed directions to the visitors' homes. These maps are inserted into a coffee mug that contains information about our church. The mugs are then placed on shelves by zip code. After each worship service, we have another team of volunteers committed to a particular zip code who pick up the mugs and deliver them within 48 hours.

By the end of worship on Sunday evening, all of our visitors will be "mugged."

We use a specialty printing company to supply our mugs. Each year we select a theme to imprint on the mug, which also includes the name of our church and the year. When we first started the church, we would order extra mugs and sell them to our members for up to twice the actual cost of the mug. Our members loved having the current year's mug, and they knew that by purchasing the mug they were helping to ensure that a visitor would get a mug. Currently, we purchase mugs as a part of our annual stewardship drive. Each family who makes a commitment to the annual stewardship campaign receives a coffee mug with the year as a small token of appreciation. The remainder of the mugs are used for first-time visitors.

For the first five years our church existeed, Adam did all that I am about to describe. After worship each week, he would tear off the sheets with the names of the visitors. He would go home from church and have lunch with his wife and daughters. Then in the afternoon, usually with one of his daughters in tow, he would deliver coffee mugs to all of the people who had visited the church for the first time that weekend. He would knock on the door and in many cases the person would have this look on their face like, *"Oh my gosh! What is the pastor doing here?"* And he would say, *"Don't worry. I don't want to come in. But, I wanted you to know how glad I am that you and your family visited our church today. Thank you so much for coming. I have a small gift for you; this is a coffee mug with our church's name on it. I would like you to have that as a gift. And we want it to be a reminder that we would love to be your church family. There is a little more information about our church inside. Do you have any questions?"* And if there were none, Adam would say goodbye and leave. If the visitor wasn't home, Adam would write a personal note, put it inside the mug and leave it by the door. The visits didn't take long at all, and a coffee mug isn't something that gets easily tossed out. Every time that visitor opens up the kitchen cabinet, he or she is going to see our church name there on the shelf.

If a family that Adam had visited returned the next week, he would immediately welcome them by name. Now, here's something very important:

If Adam could call visitors by name on their second visit to our church, they were more likely to become a part of our congregation. It meant something to them that the senior pastor took the time to learn their names. You see evangelism is about relationships. It's about people. And remembering names is important.

Adam is not personally able to deliver all the mugs anymore. We have a team of volunteers who deliver these mugs, but the idea and value of following up with visitors is still one of the keys to our church's growth. To help us remember names, we encourage our members to wear nametags to all church events. We make sure nametags are available at all meetings, Bible studies, and events. We want to do all we can to call a person by his or her name.

Third Visit Follow-up

After a visitor has visited three times, we take a next step at connection. During the first five years of the church, Adam would personally phone individuals or families after their third visit. He would contact them and thank them for visiting the church and ask if he could drop by their home for 30 minutes. He would use this time to get to know the individual or family more, share his own personal faith story, and share information about the church. At the close of that time, Adam would pray for them. Many times at the close of the prayer, he would notice tears streaming down a person's face. For many of them, it was the first time someone had prayed aloud for them as an adult.

During that visit, we became their church family because Adam took the time to listen and to develop a relationship. He may not have led them to Christ yet, but what he had done was build a relationship that would lead them toward Christ. In the first five years of the church, Adam made 500 of these visits to people in their homes. Only one of those families didn't join. All the rest joined our church. It is not possible for Adam to do this personally anymore, due to our size. Our well-trained volunteers deliver mugs to first-time visitors and our Connection Team personally calls or sends letters to third-time visitors.

If coffee mugs are not in your budget, consider a gift of bread, cookies, a candle, or something else to say, "Thank you for coming." Follow-up with first-time visitors needs to be a priority for your church in order to grow and thrive. When asked about the most important thing Adam did to help the church grow in the first five years, Adam always answers, "Delivering coffee mugs and doing in-home visits." This is still the most effective means of helping bring visitors to Christ.

Bill Easum, church consultant and author, reinforces the idea of the importance of the senior pastor doing this first-time visitor follow-up. He says in his article "How to Grow a Church Under 500 in Worship,"

> "I used to teach that lay people should make the first visit with newcomers. I was wrong. I knew in my gut I was wrong but everyone seemed to believe it to be true and even backed it up with studies. But it wasn't true in my history. It wasn't true in pastors like Adam Hamilton or Michael Slaughter, or Randy Frazee, or. . . . I can go on and on with a list of pastors who grew their small church by personal one-on-one evangelism with visitors who showed up at church.
>
> So you can begin, pastor, by making in-person calls on first-time visitors within twenty-four hours after they attend and eighty-five percent of them will return the following week. If this home visit is made within seventy-two hours, sixty percent of them return. If it is made more than seven days later, fifteen percent return. You see, the average person today visits several churches before deciding on a church home. This means they may not come back for six weeks. By then, they decide which church to return to by the friendliness and helpfulness of the members. If you wait until they return the second time, you lose eighty-five percent of your visitors."

Effective follow-up applies to program ministries as well. We have follow-up strategies for visitors to children's ministries, student ministries, and adult ministries. Even if you are a church member attending a program for the "first time," we follow up to make sure to ask about your experience and to encourage you to return. Once you have become a member, if you miss worship four times in a row, we have a team of volunteers who will try to connect with you through a phone call that week. We want people to know that they are missed, and to encourage them to return to worship, or to provide care for them should we discover something has occurred in their personal lives that is preventing them from attending church.

Connection Team

Easy access to information about your church is important to a visitor. Having a central location has been a very effective way for visitors to quickly spot where they can go to get information on weekends. However, we have discovered that many will come in during the week, so we keep our connection area staffed with a volunteer not only during each worship service, but also during weekdays. We want to make certain we are able to connect with as many people as possible.

The Connection Point volunteers are well-trained. They know the history of the church and are prepared to answer many basic questions about ministries and programs. They know how to access information from the Web site to answer questions, and they also know how to contact a ministry leader or staff person to get additional information if needed. Ministry brochures are attractive and displayed in a location where they are easily accessed. Our goal is that all material is written to reach a non and nominally religious person, someone new to our church or new to getting connected. We also make it a point to walk a visitor to the location of a class, program, or event they may be inquiring about versus just pointing the way.

Each of our ministry areas is intentional about finding ways that a new person can connect easily and quickly into their ministries. In adult discipleship we launch new small groups, new Bible studies, new classes, and new service projects regularly so that a person never has to wait to get connected into something starting new. Our children and student ministry areas also have easy, ongoing entry points for new children and new youth to get connected quickly. Assimilating into the life of the church as quickly as possible is key to retaining visitors.

Timely follow-up is a high value at our church. We ask all our staff and ministry leaders to return phone calls and e-mails within 24 hours. We are also intentional about using out-of-office responses on voice-mail and e-mail so that anyone who contacts us is able to know when a follow-up reply might be expected.

What additional motivation is needed? God genuinely cares about your visitors, and I can think of no greater motivator to inspire excellent follow-up and connection procedures. If I were to visit your church for the first time this Sunday, do you have a plan to follow up with me and help me get connected? Or will I be "released"?

Chapter Five
Helping Individuals on Their Journey

But grow in the grace and knowledge of our Lord and Savior Jesus Christ.
—2 Peter 3:18a

I had the blessing of growing up within a close driving distance to my great-grandparents' 200-acre farm in southwest Missouri, deep in the Ozark Mountains. During visits, my great-grandfather would grab his cane fishing pole and invite me to follow him to the pond for an afternoon of fishing for our evening meal. During these fishing trips, he would invite me to sit on the bank of the pond while he baited his hook with the big earthworm we had dug up by the garden and put in an old coffee can. He would fish, and I would watch. I watched how he baited the hook; I watched how he cast the line in the pond; I watched how he took notice of the action of the red bobber; and I watched how he reeled in the fish. I did a lot of watching. I enjoyed sitting on the bank watching him fish; it was comfortable, and my great-grandfather was a good teacher. One day, after many visits to the pond, he handed me a baited hook and said, "I want to make you a fisherman." He was calling me from sitting on the bank of the pond, to a higher level of participation. He was inviting me to learn to fish.

As churches, we sometime have a tendency to allow our congregants to sit in the pew weekend after weekend listening to great sermons, but never calling them to respond. We don't ask them to take that step from sitting in the pew to a higher level of participation and commitment in their walk with Christ.

In Mark 1:16-19 Jesus invites the disciples to follow him and learn to fish for people. He called them to a high level of commitment—to leave behind all that they had, to follow him, and to be fully active in ministry, growing in their relationship with him. As churches, we must find ways to inspire those who have yet to make a commitment to take a next step, to know, love, and serve God.

Invitation to Join

At Church of the Resurrection we host a gathering we call Coffee with the Pastor. It is designed to invite visitors to take their next step, to make a commitment to be fully engaged in the life of the church and in growing in their faith. We want to make sure that visitors have an opportunity to ask questions about the church and hear the stories of who we are and what we're about. This is meant to be an intentional focus on helping visitors find their place in our community.

Coffee with the Pastor is held a minimum of six times a year, typically on Sunday afternoon from 2:00 to 4:00 pm. We offer childcare, and anyone is welcome to attend. We make a special point to invite those who have visited three times or more by sending a personal letter or e-mail, but we also put an open invitation in the weekly worship bulletin and the weekly e-note, and we offer invitations from the pulpit. The invitation is for anyone who is interested in learning more about our church or who would like more information about how to move from visitor to member.

As the visitors arrive at our chapel, they are greeted by a great team of volunteers who serve as hosts for the event. Each family is handed a folder of information and a clipboard with a membership form. The information folder contains rochures about the church, our ministry programs including information on children and youth, stewardship information, a commitment card, and a form where they can immediately sign up for their next step in discipleship and connection. We also include a form asking for the first and last name of each family member, and we gather these forms from them before the presentation begins. We use the information to create nametags that we hand out to everyone at the conclusion of the Coffee even if they don't decide to become a member.

One of the executive team members welcomes the group from the platform and then invites the visitors to greet one another. After this time of greeting, attention is directed to the agenda and we explain that for the next hour they will hear more about our church. At the end of the hour, they will be given the opportunity to join the church. Of course, we also assure the group that should they decide they are not ready to make a commitment to membership, we still welcome them and want to be their church family.

At this point, our pastor leads the presentation. This is his opportunity to connect with the visitors, and it is a chance for them to get to know him better. During the next hour, Adam shares with them his story of how he came to faith in Christ and how Christ has transformed his life. He shares the story of the church so that they can better understand our purpose and vision. He shares where we see the church going in the future. He shares our four expectations of membership and then opens the room to answer specific questions from the visitors.

We also take time to introduce the Congregational Care Team. We explain that as a community of faith, we have a team of people who are there to support and care for all of our church family. We want our visitors to know that we have a team of people who will visit them in the hospital, pray with them, and care for them when they have special concerns.

Finally, we close by giving them the opportunity to make a decision to become a member. We pray and ask for God's guidance as our visitors discern whether this is the church God would have them join. After prayer, we dismiss for ten minutes and invite everyone to share in fellowship with coffee, lemonade, and cookies. Additional staff and volunteer leaders from the various ministries in the church are on hand during this time to answer questions. Those who make a decision to join are invited back into the chapel for a ten minute joining service. For those who are still undecided, we remind them that regardless of whether they decide to become a member, we will still be their church family. They are welcome to join at any future Coffee with the Pastor and they can make their commitment when they choose.

The brief joining service includes reciting the Apostles' Creed, and asking the following questions:

1) Do you wish to be a disciple and follower of Jesus Christ?
2) Will you make this your church family, allowing the people of this church

to love and care for you, as together we serve God with our prayers, presence, gifts, and service?

At the conclusion, we welcome them officially as members. The new members complete the membership paperwork received in their packet of information and take this membership form to a table in the narthex where they meet their Congregational Care pastor personally and pick up their nametags. Each family gets their picture taken so we can include it with their information in our database. At times, we have also posted these pictures with the family's name on a bulletin board in our narthex under the heading of Welcome New Members. It is important that not only our pastors and staff have the opportunity to meet them, but we want our congregation to welcome them as well. The weekend following the Coffee with the Pastor, we will announce how many new members have joined the church and invite any of the new members attending that worship service to stand. Our congregation will officially welcome them, normally with applause. Our pastor explains that the people standing have made a commitment to become members at Church of the Resurrection. In return, he asks those who are members to make a commitment to be their church family, and the congregation responds, "We will." We then offer a prayer of thanksgiving for our new members.

We take two additional steps to help our members get acquainted with the new members. At the beginning and end of worship, we scroll all the new members' names on the video screens. In the past we typed them on special inserts that we placed in our weekend bulletins but just recently moved to scrolling them on the screens. In Adam's weekly e-mail to the congregation, he mentions how many new people joined the church and then shares their names in the e-mail. Our congregation is encouraged to look through the list to see if there is someone they may know and to be certain to welcome them by name. He also invites the congregation to pray for all of the new members by name.

Membership Expectations

While membership is not required to participate in the life of our church, we want to encourage visitors to move toward membership and grow in their faith walk and deepen their connection to the community of faith. We are sure to communicate that we will be their church either way. We'll visit them in the hospital, do their weddings and funerals, and they are able to participate in all of our programs. We even make nametags for our visitors that look like our member nametags.

Some churches downplay any expectations for new members. They are often afraid that visitors will be turned off by requiring anything of them. At our church, we think the opposite. We think people are looking for something to commit to. We think that visitors are looking for a place to belong. We talk about membership like it's a marriage. It's a sign of commitment. People understand that when they get married they bring something to the relationship as well as get something out of it. When you commit to a church in this way, you feel responsible for her; you commit to her purpose, vision, and ministry.

So, we're clear from the very beginning that with membership there are expectations involved. For instance, when visitors become members they will no longer be able to park in the closer parking spaces we set aside for our visitors. Instead, they are asked like all our other members to park in the farthest away spots. If they join they will receive the annual stewardship mailings, including a pledge card. If they join, they will be called upon to serve inside and outside the walls of the church.

Many times, this part of the discussion moves visitors toward membership. They want their membership to mean something. They want to become more committed to Christ and the church. The fact that membership is about responsibilities and expectations, not privileges and benefits, makes it all the more compelling.

We expect that our members attend worship every weekend unless they are sick or out of town. We expect that our members will grow in their faith apart from worship, ideally participating in a small group. Members are encouraged to read Scripture and pray daily as a way of growing in their faith. We expect that our members will serve God at least once within the walls of the church, and a minimum of ten hours per year outside the walls of the church.

God has called us to be salt and light in the world, and one way we do that is by serving others and sharing Christ. We ask that all members find a meaningful way to serve. They may be willing to make a weekly commitment as an usher, greeter, children's ministry leader, choir member, or they may make a monthly commitment to greeting, data entry, mugging, and many other opportunities. We also provide ways to make a shorter-term commitment such as handing out candles at Christmas Eve, stuffing bulletins once a month, or sorting food after the annual Souper Bowl food drive. All members are also asked to serve outside the walls of the church in the community or in the world. We keep all service opportunities posted on our Web site with clearly communicated contact information so they can get connected easily and quickly.

We also expect that our members give in proportion to their income with the tithe being the goal. Commitment to generosity is an important step on the journey to know, love, and serve God. The Bible teaches us to give a tithe, or the first 10 percent of what we earn, to God and God's work. We understand that 10 percent is a goal for some and a starting point for others. We explain that when they return a portion of their resources to God through their tithes and offerings, they are investing in God's vision and mission, and they create an opportunity for God to work through them and through our church.

Recognizing that it is human nature to become complacent, each fall our senior pastor preaches a series of sermons aimed at reminding our members of all of these expectations and inspiring them to take their next steps in growing in their faith and commitment to Christ. In addition, all of our program ministries are required to clearly communicate how a person's participation in their particular ministry or program will help them grow in their journey to know, love, and serve God.

Knowing, Loving, and Serving God—The Journey of Discipleship
The Christian life is not meant to be lived alone. We were created for connection—with God and with one another. By now you can probably recite our purpose statement: "To build a Christian community where non and nominally religious people are becoming deeply committed Christians." You have read that everything we do is guided by our purpose statement and is measured against the purpose statement. You have read about all the ways we are intentional in our outreach strategies, our emphasis and attention to detail and a commitment to do "whatever it takes," the way we design worship

services, and the value we have placed on radical hospitality in order to help us reach unchurched persons in our community. You have read about our intentional follow-up strategies and the way we invite people to take make a greater commitment. But what is our end goal? Where are we taking people?

At Resurrection, we have defined a deeply committed Christian as someone who loves God with his or her head, or is being theologically informed, loves God with his or her heart, or is being spiritually transformed, and serves God with his or her hands in the world. We call this, *Our Journey: Knowing, Loving, and Serving God.*

For many of the congregants whether visitor or member, we recognize that they are at different places on their journey. We know that each day they are faced with decisions, demands, and converging pathways where they have to decide what is most important and which direction to take. We don't want their faith journey to be that complicated, so we developed a simple pathway to help them get connected easily on the journey to know, love, and serve God. We want them to say "yes" to the amazing journey that God has planned for them!

For many, worship is that first step. The next step is to participate in one of our specially designed learning communities. Community is where we connect and explore the faith with others who are also on the journey. It's the place where we begin to examine Christianity, study the Bible, and discover what it means to know, love, and serve God.

Four learning communities make up our initial steps into community. First, we encourage those who are interested in an overview of the Christian faith or who are uncertain where to begin, to start with the Alpha course. We especially promote Alpha to those who are exploring Christianity, but we have also discovered that those who have been Christians for years also receive great benefit from starting their journey of connection with Alpha. In addition to Alpha, we offer three other Learning Communities, focused around *Knowing God, Loving God, and Serving God.*

Knowing God

This six-week learning community explores the good news of the Bible and helps the participants discover study tools and resources to deepen their understanding of the Scripture. Because we are reaching so many non and nominally religious people, many have no basic knowledge of the Bible, how it is organized, or how to use it. So, we offer a basic Bible class to set the foundation for faith formation.

Loving God

During this six week learning community, we introduce participants to spiritual practices that will help participants grow in their relationship with God and others. Each session focuses on a different practice and each participant leaves with a practical way to experience it during the week. When they gather again the following week, they discuss their experience with the practice.

Serving God

In this course, people discover spiritual gifts and what it means to serve others on the journey. They explore stewardship of time and financial resources. We also cover the basics of evangelism and faith sharing as well.

At Resurrection, we believe one of the best ways to nurture a growing relationship with Jesus Christ is to belong to a small group of Christian friends who encourage, challenge, and support one another as each person discerns and lives out his or her life mission. We have a dedicated team that helps our congregants find a group that is best suited for them based on where they live, their interests, or their life situation. Small groups are the place where care, support, Bible study, fellowship, and service is lived out. Most of our small groups meet off-campus in the group members' homes, but we do have some groups, primarily Sunday morning groups, that meet on campus. This affords them the ability to access childcare on campus.

Our database is one of our key resources when it comes to connecting people to small groups. We keep data on which people in our congregation are in a small group and to which group they belong. We tag each person's small group information into their data record so that as needed, we can access this information. For instance, the first thing we do when we are notified that someone has experienced the death of someone close or is going into the hospital is to see if that person is in a small group. If so, the small group is notified and becomes the source of support for meals, visits, and prayer for the individual. We normally find that the small group is already way ahead of us in their care of their group members.

For those who are not ready for a small group because of personal or emotional needs, we have a pathway for them to experience authentic Christian care and connection through small groups in one of our support groups or the Celebrate Recovery program. Each week Celebrate Recovery meets to help those who are dealing with hurts, hang-ups, or habits. Through worship, fellowship, connection with others, and caring facilitation they experience the love of Christ leading them to wholeness and healing. Ministries like Celebrate Recovery and the many other support groups are great outreach ministries attracting people in the community who do not have a church home.

The Journey Continues. . . .

By now you know just about everything there is to know about how we fish for people at Church of the Resurrection. After we have done all we can do to get people in our doors, we want to invite them to become a part of something bigger than themselves. Yes, we want them to choose us as their church home, but more than that, we want them to become deeply committed Christians. We want them to use their gifts and experience to serve others and to develop friendships along the way while serving in our local community, the world abroad, or within the walls of our church.

We are all on this journey together. It's important that visitors and new members understand that they are stepping into the journey at whatever point in their faith they may be. Each person in our church is at a different point—whether children who are learning to know, love, and serve God in their own way; or teenagers who are learning to unleash their faith in God; or adults at various stages in their lives—we share the journey together no matter our starting point. Our invitation is to begin the journey toward a deeply committed relationship with Jesus Christ.

Jesus' disciples didn't hesitate to follow him when he called them from the shore. I think his message must have been so compelling that there was no way they were going to pass up the opportunity to experience this journey of a lifetime. Our churches need to inspire people to drop everything and follow Jesus. We can do all of the effective marketing techniques and get visitors flooding our doors, but if we don't inspire them to know, love, and serve God, what have we really accomplished? Inspiring, consistent, and clear messaging is important as you guide people in their next steps of discipleship.

How are you calling visitors from the "shore" and inviting them to discover more about what it means to follow Jesus?

Afterword
The Joy of Finding Strays and Fishing for People

by Adam Hamilton

In your local community it is likely that at least 50 percent of the people are not active in a church family. Often they consider themselves "spiritual but not religious." These are our children and grandchildren, nieces and nephews. How does God look at these non-religious people? What does God expect churches to do in order to reach out to them?

A passage of Scripture that seems pivotal in Jesus' ministry and must therefore inform our work as churches is Ezekiel 34. Through the prophet Ezekiel, God speaks to the civic and religious leaders of the Jewish people and says,

> Woe to the shepherds of Israel who only take care of themselves! Should not shepherds take care of the flock? You eat the curds, clothe yourselves with the wool and slaughter the choice animals, but you do not take care of the flock. You have not strengthened the weak or healed the sick or bound up the injured. You have not brought back the strays or searched for the lost. You have ruled them harshly and brutally. So they were scattered because there was no shepherd, and when they were scattered they became food for all the wild animals. My sheep wandered over all the mountains and on every high hill. They were scattered over the whole earth, and no one searched or looked for them. I myself will search for my sheep and look after them. As a shepherd looks after his scattered flock when he is with them, so will I look after my sheep. I will rescue them from all the places where they were scattered on a day of clouds and darkness. I will bring them out from the nations and gather them from the countries, and I will bring them into their own land. I will pasture them on the mountains of Israel, in the ravines and in all the

71

settlements in the land. I will tend them in a good pasture, and the mountain heights of Israel will be their grazing land. There they will lie down in good grazing land, and there they will feed in a rich pasture on the mountains of Israel. I myself will tend my sheep and have them lie down, declares the Sovereign Lord. I will search for the lost and bring back the strays. I will bind up the injured and strengthen the weak, but the sleek and the strong I will destroy. I will shepherd the flock with justice. (Ezekiel 34: 2-5, 11-16)

I believe it was this passage that Jesus had in mind when he said *"I am the good shepherd"* (John 10:11). Matthew noted that when Jesus looked at the multitudes he had compassion on them because they were *"like sheep without a shepherd"* (Matthew 9:36). Jesus devoted most of his time to seeking to minister to people who were lost sheep. I believe he was revealing his own heart when he spoke of the shepherd who had one hundred sheep, but who left the ninety-nine behind to *"go after the [one] lost sheep until he finds it"* (Luke 15:4). The text goes on to say that when he has found the sheep *"he joyfully puts it on his shoulders and goes home. Then he calls his friends and neighbors together and says, 'Rejoice with me; I have found my lost sheep.' I tell you that in the same way there will be more rejoicing in heaven over one sinner who repents than over ninety-nine righteous persons who do not need to repent"* (Luke 15:5-7). Notice the prevalence of joy that comes in finding lost sheep!

Another metaphor Jesus used is that of a fisher. He saw himself as a man fishing for people. His fishing was "catch and release." Imagine Jesus catching fish from a small pond filled with scum and silt and algae and then releasing them into the deep and fresh waters of the Kingdom of God. Jesus' call to his first disciples and still to us today is, *"Come, follow me. . . and I will send you out to fish for people"* (Mark 1:16-18).

As I've been writing this chapter I've been sitting by a pond where a friend of mine brought his four-and-a-half year old grandson to fish. They've carefully chosen the right spot to fish (into the wind) and have brought a variety of lures to try. They cast their lines into the water and slowly reel them in. Most of the time they catch nothing, but today the fish are biting. And every ten minutes or so either the boy or his grandfather shouts, "I've got one, I've got one!"

Talk about joy! It doesn't get any better than this for a grandfather and his grandson.

The mission of our churches is to continue the mission of Jesus. We are meant to continue the search for lost sheep. We are meant to continue to fish for people. And there is incredible joy in finding lost sheep and in fishing for people.

I got in my car Sunday after church and found that someone had left a note on my seat that read, "Pastor Adam, thank you for leading a church that would change the course of my life over the years. How I dated, how I treat my wife, how I now raise my son—these are all different because I became a Christian here in this church. I am eternally grateful."

I felt joy in reading his note, but the note itself expressed the joy this man had found in meeting and following the Good Shepherd and from swimming in God's seas.

This book was written to encourage you as you seek to lead your church to "bring back the strays and search for the lost." It is a guide to fishing for people. But finding the strays and fishing for people is not merely about technique; it is about cultivating a love for lost sheep and discovering the joy of fishing for people.

After an hour of fishing, Drake and his grandpa are heading home. They caught twelve fish altogether today. Their hands were a bit smelly and their bodies were a bit sweaty—this happens when you're fishing. But as the boy walked to the car he turned to me and said, "That was **AWESOME!**"

As your congregation rediscovers the joy of fishing, and they begin to see people's lives changed through the ministry of your church, I suspect you'll hear them say, "That was **AWESOME!**"

Adam Hamilton
June 1, 2009

NOTES

NOTES

NOTES

NOTES

NOTES

NOTES